Elegy for Joseph Cornell

María Negroni

ELEGY FOR
JOSEPH CORNELL

Translated from the Spanish by Allison A. deFreese

DALKEY ARCHIVE PRESS

McLean, IL / Dublin

Originally published by Caja Negra Editores as *Elegía Joseph Cornell* in 2013

Copyright © by María Negroni in 2019

Translation copyright © by Allison A. deFreese, 2019.

First Dalkey Archive edition, 2020.

CIP Data available on request.

www.dalkeyarchive.com

McLean, IL / Dublin

Printed on permanent/durable acid-free paper.

Acknowledgements

The image from *Children's Party* by Joseph Cornell is reprinted with permission of the Anthology Film Archives. Other sources cited include: "Our Angelic Ancestor" from Charles Simic's *Dime-store Alchemy* (translated into Spanish by María Negroni under the title *Totemismo y otros poemas*); Leonie Peters' "Philosophical Toys: play, collecting and experience in the art of Joseph Cornell;" Richard Howard's "An Aporia for Joseph Cornell; Stanley Kunitz' "The Crystal Cage," Robert Coover's *The Grand Hotels* (of Joseph Cornell) and fragments from Dore Ashton's *A Joseph Cornell Album.*

Several of my translations from *Elegy for Joseph Cornell* have previously appeared in *Apofenie, Asymptote, Burningwood, CAGIBI,* and *Solstice.*

I would like to thank María Negroni, my mother, Michael, Cecilia López-Flores, and John O'Brien for their consultations and feedback on the translation; my gratitude also to the Multnomah County Library, as well as the MHCC, CCC and Reed College libraries for their comprehensive ILL services.

Contents

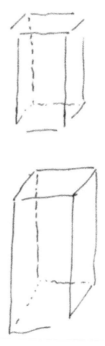

Joseph Cornell's
Boxes

—thrift-shop

dioramas—

Prologue

Joseph Cornell
inside your boxes
my words become visible
for a moment.
Octavio Paz

as though the body is a box
which holds the heart and is
crowded with absence.
Susan Wood

I DON'T KNOW when or where I first saw Joseph Cornell's boxes. Both the MOMA and Guggenheim have several of his pieces in their permanent collections and, believe it or not, I visited both museums every week when I settled in New York in the late 80s. What I do remember is that his art, as well as his persona as a solitary wanderer, fascinated me instantly with the force of a fixed idea.

Above all, what drew me to Cornell was his imagery rooted in the nineteenth century—his love of divas and ballerinas; Novalis and Rimbaud; Berlioz and Emily Dickinson; of urban debris and *artificialia*; maps and dreams; soap bubbles and toys; hotels, and the extremely literal. But undoubtedly, what truly seduced me at the time—because I, too, never stopped exploring it—was Cornell's relationship with the city. His enthusiasm for reinventing Manhattan as a cabinet of curiosities, as a privileged place from which, under the guise of anonymity, you may observe and plunder, which is the same thing as opening yourself to infinite versions of the world and, above all, yourself.

You will tell me this idea already exists in Baudelaire's work, and that is true. But Cornell (1903-1972) captures a different kind of center. For his imaginary map, you need only confine yourself to a radius that begins and ends in Times Square. Manhattan is the image machine he combed through and which he reassembled through his obsession. A universe that offers itself up, in miniature, and with the lavishness of a labyrinth, with innumerable doors, both visible and hidden, which bring to mind the beautiful divine palace of the Kabbalists or the *catastrophe féerique* imagined by Le Corbusier.

What I mean is that Manhattan was the homeland of Cornell's imagination. It was there that he conceived the ideas for his boxes, assembling them in a rambling fashion like poetic theaters in which you could stay and live. It was there that he wandered, in no particular direction, allowing himself to drift—losing himself in shops that sold old books, the dime stores of 14th Street, flea markets—as if he were a detective on the trail of the undecipherable.

Contrary to popular belief; however, Cornell was not a surrealist but rather an eccentric. Someone who, every morning, dazed by headaches and insomnia, would leave his house on Utopia Parkway (Queens)—where he lived all his life with his mother and a paralytic brother—to search for "things" that would later on allow him to create a catalogue of the unusual. Also, sometimes what he would find were films—usually B movies or low budget films—that he would later draw from for his work, using graphing and collage techniques, with the intention of giving them back, like his boxes, as *veduta* or sentimental memorabilia. Over time, his interest in movies increased, leading Cornell, who disliked shooting film, to work with several experimental cinematographers from the New York vanguard (Stan Brakhage and Rudy Burckhardt, for instance) whom he gave precise instructions regarding what and how to film.

As it happened, neither his collaborative short films nor his own cinematographic works were screened often in New York. I, too, waited almost a decade before discovering this treasure (the occasion: A retrospective organized by the Anthology Film Archives). Need I say his arrow pieced me a second time? That his films seemed a celebration of childhood lost? A repertoire of sad joys for the inconsolable?

If there are traces of my long and secret conversations with Cornell's boxes in my previous books, *Dark Museum* and *Small, Illustrated World* (and also in my translation of Dime Store Alchemy, a book Charles Simic wrote in honor of the artist), then the text that you, the reader, now have in your hands may serve as a record of my encounters with his films. Specifically, my new exploration begins with this film image: The little girl who passes by us, naked, atop a white steed, her hair covering her body as if she were a miniature, unsettling, version of Lady Godiva (this image appears in his film *Children's Trilogy*).

Cornell seems to suggest that Art is always reading an inner book that speaks about the city of the soul. It is a city containing the most usual of things: Circus magicians, Halloween parties, mischievous pranks, parks covered in snow, pigeons above equestrian statues and even busts of Mozart watching everything from a storefront window on Mulberry Street. And also, in some of his creations or temporary landscapes, a secret light that allows the marvelous to exist within the labyrinth that keeps it hidden. Then, the book closes, the city dreams, the center fades away; and the world that remains is an intangible vision—terrifying and magnificent.

María Negroni

Notes on the Translation: A Text on the Edge

ELEGY FOR JOSEPH CORNELL is at once a monologue, a collection of metafictional microfictions; a series of prose poems; an artist's quest; the hero's journey; a filmography, biography, bibliography and inventory; a travel scrapbook and a guidebook for creativity. Argentinian writer María Negroni transcends form and genre as she explores, with results both luminous and illuminating, the life of Joseph Cornell, a solitary urban artist whose work also defied conventional classification.

Neither Cornell's work nor Negroni's words fit, quite literally, into predictable "boxes." Both Cornell and Negroni are innovators and inventers in their respective media; sounding the depths of surrealism and romanticism; modernism and the Victorian era; esotericism and "camp;" sentimentality and melancholy; while approaching work and creation as play. Negroni uses literary fragments, news clippings and found poetry to create a uniquely initiated portrait of the New York artist whose work remained largely unrecognized or hidden during his lifetime.

In "Homebody," a prose poem reimagined as a dictionary entry in *Elegy for Joseph Cornell*, Negroni refers to Cornell as "an unmarked player" and "[s]omeone who transforms the unattainable into his purest passion not because pursuit of the unattainable prevents him from achieving a real emotional life, but precisely because the unattainable is what nourishes it." Of the children bobbing for apples in "(*Cotillion*, 1940)" she writes: "Joseph Cornell works here, on that edge," an edge where a boy lets an apple fall from his mouth "so he can keep playing," an edge that tests the elastic boundaries between the work and play. In other poems, Negroni depicts Cornell's work as a "festival of sad childhood" or perhaps a "celebration of childhood lost." She describes his early endeavors in experimental filmmaking as "a game, after all, like all works of art" and his collages as a medium that "succeeds in letting the imagination play games, encouraging cracks to form in the world; suspending reason, once again, to the benefit of desire." This is a view that Cornell himself appears to have shared in his lifetime, having written: "Shadow boxes become poetic theater or settings wherein are metamorphosed the elements of a childhood pastime."

In her homage to an artist who continually explored the edge of art and culture, María Negroni, too, examines borders throughout *Elegy*— through form as well as via a fragmented narrative framed in unexpected ways. As the young girl from Cornell's *Children's Trilogy* (who serves as narrator or chorus throughout the book while "brandishing a transparent secret") informs the reader: "I have no time to play outside these words." Through the persona of "small Amazon," Negroni examines another edge—inviting a connection between early vestiges of Western feminism (Godgifu or Godiva as "Good Eve," a champion for female sexuality) and the secret world of an omnipotent child performer or child "star" crossing the sky. In Joseph Cornell, María Negroni finds an ally in myth revisionism, a source for creating new stories of a matriarchal universe:

> In the beginning, the Goddess of All Things arose, naked, from the Chaos . . . [She] laid a silver egg from which the universe emerged. . . . She was known as Wander without Limits or Brilliant Mother of Nothing, worshipped as Visible Moon in her three phases: as a damsel or girl, as a lusty nymph and as a soothsaying crone. So the girl on the white steed could be Isis or Ishtar or Iphigenia or even Helen of the Tree or the *pétite Héloïse*. . .

The child rider steers her own steed through galaxies that span the primordial past, while imagining a spellbinding present ("with one foot in eternity and the other in mud"). She ultimately chooses her own destiny in María Negroni's interpretation of Cornell's dreamscape fairytale.

"All translation is a kind of illusion," André Lefevere once said, and these translations bridge the impossible illusion that one language may be rendered through the words of another, providing a point of entry into worlds both real and imaginary. After all, according to Negroni's tiny Godiva, "borders do not exist, and all acts of fleeing are an illusion." The presence of ambiguity or perceived "illusion" in art clears a channel for discussion. And in an era when the very basis of reality and fact are increasingly under question, perhaps today, more than ever, we need a space for questioning at the margins. We need more uncertainty, more room for interpretation and play, a chance to "discover a form based on an absence of form," as María Negroni suggests, and to create, or "make a mortal leap into the impossible." According to Charles Simic (whose book *Dime-store Alchemy*, also about Joseph Cornell, Negroni translated into Spanish), "even in this claim that to translate poetry is impossible, I find an ideal situation. Poetry itself is about the impossible. All arts are about doing the impossible."

Modernist Brooklyn poet Marianne Moore, with whom "magical illusionist" Cornell maintained a correspondence for many years, describes "imaginary gardens with real toads in them." In such gardens we may find Cornell's shadowboxes and films cropped from found footage or Negroni's "infinite versions of the world—and above all, of yourself." Just as the areas of a biome that have the greatest biodiversity are often found on the edges—the borderlands where two ecosystems overlap; the space where a meadow meets a forest or the freshwater river finds the ocean; or else openings in the ice that allow water and other elements to mingle, and birds to survive the winter—so too in Cornell and Negroni's worlds we find an environment where creativity, ideas and innovative artists may flourish.

Allison A. deFreese

Elegy for Joseph Cornell

e

l   *e*
   g   *í*   *a*

                    j
                         o
                  s
                    e
                         p
              h

         c
              o
      r
   n
      e
           l

           l

el-e-gy \ ˈe-lə-jē\ *n, pl* **–gies** [L elegia poem in elegiac cou-
plets, fr. Gk *elegeia, elegeion,* fr. *elegos* song of mourning]
(1501) **1:** a poem in elegiac couplets **2a** : a song or poem
expressing sorrow or lamentation esp. for one who is dead
b: something (as a speech) resembling such a song or poem
3a : a short pensive or reflective poem that is usually nostalgic
or melancholy **b:** a short pensive musical composition

Joseph Cornell, *Children's Party*.

Joseph Cornell, *Children's Party*

Childhood is greatly needed. Those endless days of mysterious alliteration, and those endless nights of stillness—with no more movement than the false calm of the clocks—are needed. A little girl, naked, drifts past on a white steed. A young prince dressed as a scarecrow is spying on her. Everything feeds the void: Life is reading a poem, somewhat obscene, about Life.

(*Cotillion*, 1940)

Children are false models, unfinished stories. Here they are in a 1950s dining room at a party, surrounded by balloons, paper horns, and streamers. Soon they will: Fish a floating apple from a metal tub, using their teeth; fall asleep; drink sodas or pin the tail on the donkey—their gestures somewhat untidy. A child always brings his own piece of the world into the world so that reality exists. One might feel afraid of his white ankle socks, and of his vitality, which borders on cruelty. Joseph Cornell works here, on that edge where the apple is about to fall from the boy's mouth—so he can keep playing. All through life, this same gesture: Capturing and losing, capturing and losing. The child a lonely hunter: His heart eludes him, and in that absence, destiny conspires; immensity is illuminated.

λλλλλ λλλλλλ

λλλ λλλλλ λλλλλ λλλλλ

λλλλλ λλλλλ λλλλλ λλλλλ λλλλλ

λλλλλ λλλλλ λλλλλ λλλλλ λλλλλ

λλλλλ λλλλλ λλλλλ

λλλλλλλλλ λλλλλ

λλλλλ

λλλλλ

Toward a silent poetry: To think is to guess. I do not know if I will manage to find a future idea that way, but am willing to try. The important thing now is to tend the void (without passion, travel itinerary, or attachment to anything concrete), to combine what is common with eroticism and culture. To discover a form based on an absence of form. Is this even possible? Oh! If only I could become a swirl of arabesque smoke with its rising disorder—a swarm of gods in a workshop open to incoherence, as if in an afterlife state.

(Aviary, 1955)

The scene takes place in Union Square. It is winter—almost. The camera circles, as do the birds—as do pigeons, when not eating or resting on the statues' heads.

Union Square in the 1950s was, as today, a specimen collection full of curiosities. A dwarf dressed in a suit crosses the park; a child reads poems that no one has written; a young woman waits for someone to love her, or perhaps (and this is, after all, the same thing), for someone to place her own name into her hands. Cornell's camera circles, and in white letters writes the sky's biography—the images loading from the threshold. A book with no pages ignites.

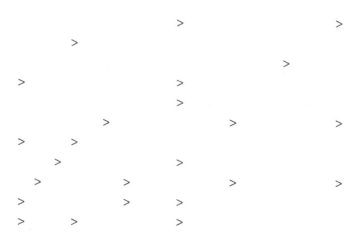

He is an artist of longings […]. He preferred the ticket to the trip, the postcard to the place, the fragment to the whole.

Adam Gopnik, *The New Yorker*

Cornell's boxes were never toys, but
rather philosophical acts of the highest order.

Louis Aragon

Gourmet art by a man who only ate junk food.

Robert Motherwell

the child

The little girl who drifts past, naked, on her white steed would have left Lewis Carroll sleepless. A fairytale castle twinkles in the background. Everything falls under the same spell: the moon is turning her head away; it is midnight at her party, the "I" leads a parade of shadows. The girl lowers her eyes, searching desperately for the well of invisibility. When she reaches the castle, a white rabbit will open the door.

Wonderlust

Objective chance was not enough for Cornell.

His secret must be enclosed, surrounded by silence, crystalized within a shrine.

Also, lightning (that baroque and surrealist *coup de foudre*) must create its own private mansion, an intimate place where found objects may reverberate in their own web of constellations.

Inside the box is where the passion for dreaming is shared—

which, in turn, stirs the Magus' greed.

He announces his Creed:

"The highest theater in the world, that's me."

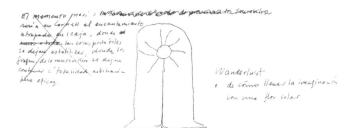

12

the stars

There is a wall. And behind this wall are stars, hidden behind still other stars. Perhaps they were once fires—high visual echoes heading into ash. Who knows, distance is dazzling, just as Novalis' odes dazzle us. Everything is happening at once—even the sky, the very low sky, where we burn—with one foot in eternity and the other in mud. The fact is that there is a wall, and real stars behind the other stars. What more is love? A girl drifts past, naked, brandishing a transparent secret.

Notes for a Short Biography

I

The man loved getting lost in the city in which he lived. He was born at 1:13 p.m. from a blue heart inside a seashell that someone left in a hotel room. We know that his mother loved playing the piano and that his father sold fabric, that several children lived in the house—including one who was paralytic—and that they all played together on Utopia Parkway. These were earthly games with the semblance of prayers—as are all games—and the children threw themselves into their play as if they were magicians or trapeze artists or flea trainers in the mythical circus of their youth. The children had grown up now, and the man worked alone in the basement. He had surrounded himself with metonymies of his own body and with them assembled small boxes that contained the world which, as you know, contains everything, even children with disabilities. Meanwhile, the city outside continued to exist—no more, no less than he did. Sometimes, his fever rose and these were wonderful days because the streets filled with increasingly ephemeral (that is, more indispensable) objects, and the man went out, cloaked in his own amazement, as if this were any moon or any ordinary language. In his mind, however, nothing had changed. The garden was crowded with teddy bears, his mother continued baking cakes, and the basement burned like a wheelchair each time his brother asked for a star—or for any other equally impossible and wonderful object.

HOMEBODY. 1. A person who prefers introspection to action and therefore lives in a castle of diurnal dreams. 2. Someone who transforms the unattainable into his purest passion not because pursuit of the unattainable prevents him from achieving a real emotional life, but precisely because the unattainable is what nourishes it. 3. In art, someone who does not belong to a specific group, who detests classifications, who considers any stance to be a prison: much like an unmarked player. 3. (fam.) A sort of autistic genius, dedicated to unlearning.

Chambre Intime

a small

Amazon

on

a

forbidden

planet

Children's Corner:
(*Jack's Dream*, 1930)

Six minutes of stop motion film reveal the dream of the little dog—Jack's dream. A dragon, with nostrils that exhale colossal bursts of smoke, is pursuing a princess through a tableau of blue wood. She hides behind the curtain, using her wits to throw him off her track, and finally camouflages herself to the point where the dragon can no longer see her.

The story is meticulously detailed, enhanced by the drawings Cornell intersperses throughout the tale: a naval vessel flees while another confronts pirates; an acrobatic performance at the bottom of the sea; miniature horses dancing to Debussy. Now you see it, now you don't. The dog dreams he is dreaming. Chance is a guided tour, and Cornell knows this well. *Colorín Colorado*—and here our story ends.

I was before you, said the girl, and I will still exist after you reach the edge of your sky, or rather, I will exist inside you, an entire Golden Age coming and going from the small sacrifices you discreetly enclosed in your boxes. I belong to a lineage of women who, in the absolute absence of clothing, create a shield that protects us from exile in the form of ideas. I do not believe in happy little girls or in inspiration that grows out of hatred. My course, though difficult, is not pitiable. I, too, seek the glass grotto where I will sleep until I am cured by death.

From Boxes to Lyrical Daydreams on Celluloid

Cornell didn't like to film. In the 1950s, several filmmakers (Stan Brakhage and Rudy Burckhardt, among others) filmed footage for him, and then edited the material, following his precise instructions. Both in these films and the ones Cornell created himself using found materials, the syntax of composition is the same: The broken montage, dramatic cuts, abrupt interjection of subtitles, and a prevalence of cuts, letters, and inverted or repeated scenes. The rest is left to improvisation (in the musical sense) and disjointed omens.

And, nonetheless, despite this formal experimentation, Cornell has never been considered more than a mere footnote to American vanguard cinema (where Peter Kubelka, Bruce Conner, Ken Jacobs, Jonas Mekas and Maya Deren appear, among others).

Certainly his lyrical documentary style, his references to the nineteenth century, and above all—especially in his in film-collages—his tireless commemoration of childhood all have much in common with Romantic-Victorian traditions . . . on the condition of adding, as an aside, that there was always something voyeuristic about Cornell's imagination. Something unsettling, even perverse. His tendency toward aesthetics, we might say, poorly conceals his affinity for women dressed like men (Hedy Lamarr, Lauren Bacall, Marlene Dietrich, Lee Miller) and, even in the atmosphere of eternity in *Halloween Party*, he does not manage to temper his fixation with the young girl, a fixation shared by Lewis Carroll and Mark Twain.

Bébé Marie. Baby Peggy.

Welcome to the visual stalls of Joseph Cornell.

Acrobatic acts come and go, as do circus routines and whole arsenals filled with broken childhoods. Don't forget to bring your hat for when the wind blows and please remain awake and asleep during the entire performance.

Notes for a Short Biography

II

He never married. He had no formal training as an artist. He never left his childhood home on Utopia Parkway.

His fragility, they say, could not conceal his will of steel.

On a typical day, he would eat chocolate-frosted donuts and sweet peaches in syrup for breakfast, and a liverwurst sandwich and butterscotch pudding for lunch. In the afternoons, he drank tea, a lot of tea, almost always served with ice cream, and he ate all kinds of cake, candy, and chocolates. Before bed, he added to this diet several pieces of cherry pie with Chantilly cream.

Nudity is an open fruit. Perhaps, if a god were to hold the girl before a fire, he could burn away her mortality. But there are no gods in this landscape. There is a castle where the parties bloom, as well as the battles, the dark-winged night and the double door that opens into an inner vision. This is no small matter. The girl comes forward, and the hair that covers her excuses her, for now, from performing the most arduous of divine duties: making love. But the hunt for love, with its moon revolutions and blood cycles, its spell of enchantment and its price, is already pursuing her. The belly of darkness, without a sound, follows fast on her heels. Death does not cast a shadow.

The Duchamp Dossier

It's a cardboard box in which, for years, Joseph Cornell collected small keepsakes from his friendship with Duchamp. The box contains 117 items of various types: The French artist's empty tobacco pouch, two cleaners for his famous white pipe, a napkin from *Horn & Hardart* (one of those automats that was all the rage in the 30's and where they almost certainly met), letters, photographs, postcards of the Mona Lisa, several yellowed notes in his handwriting, gallery posters and even dry-cleaning receipts which reveal Duchamp's unusual habit of sending everything to the dry cleaner, even socks and handkerchiefs.

The box was put on display for the first time in 1998, on the occasion of the *Joseph Cornell/Marcel Duchamp: In Resonance* exhibition held in the Philadelphia Museum of Art.

No one can explain how Cornell managed to acquire such "mementos."

Small Shrines

Traditionally associated with the female realm of curiosity, Cornell's obsession with collecting takes the form of a Romantic museum. It is true that other artists, both those preceding and following him, also made use of boxes (Robert Rauschenberg [*Scatole Personali*], Andy Warhol [*Ice Boxes*] and Bertolt Brecht [*Cabinets*], for instance), but his go beyond the private altar, if you will, unveiling a labyrinthine series that allows the imagination to roam through this serial interpretation.

Cornell also arranged the items themselves inside boxes, so that the boxes on display represent only the tip of an iceberg. After his death, in the basement where he worked there were thousands of them—each painstakingly categorized. I offer here, as example, a few highlights:

Science and Nature: Giants of the Sea, Fish Nests, The Manhattan Zoo, Snow Storms, Monarchs of the Air, Ants and Insects, Bees, Nightingales, The Power of Clouds, Sunbeams, Moonlight, The Private Life of Birds, Rainbows.

Newsreels, Documentaries, Travels: Views of the World, Magnificent Venice, The Coronation of Queen Isabel, East Indian Islands, Spanish Children, Beautiful Naples, Wall Street, Picturesque Java, Rome Falls to the Allies, The Golden West, Memories of Our Past, The Eruption of Vesuvius.

Funny Films: Children in the Water, Chimney Cleaning, Extraordinary Illusions, A Curious Discovery, The Knight of

Black Magic, A Christmas Miracle, and several French films from the time of Lumière, Méliès and Feuillade.

Cartoons and Comic Strips: Mickey's Strange Dream, Krazy Kat, Little Nemo in Slumberland.

Comedies and Melodramas: The Old Sea Dog, Bombs and Girlfriends, Love is Blond, Love and Bullets, Recently Painted, An Arabian Nightmare, Coney Island, Cupid's Blow, Laurel and Hardy on a skyscraper, The Price She Paid, The Man Who Turned to Stone, The Great Train Robbery, A Detective and Around the World, The Tide of Destiny, Two Men and a Woman.[1]

An interminable list that could be categorized under the generic (yet precise) title that follows: Trinkets and nonsense acquired in Woolworth stores.

---

[1] In 1971, the year before his death, Joseph Cornell donated his complete collection of cinematographic materials to the Anthology Film Archives (and to Jonas Mekas, the archive's director). At least 150 of these movies are from the silent film era. Incidentally, Mekas was the first to show Cornell's short films in public. The first showing was held on November 30, 1970, during the same time of year when John Kennedy was assassinated in Dallas.

Au revoir, affectueusement

Marcel

Naked, I witnessed many visions: Words came to me, as if coming into existence for the first time, climbing the ranks in a drill of the verb *to be. Sum, fui, esse.* I was a long and unknown street, full of disasters, and I saw everything in the first degree, with insect eyes. Everything was quite enormous. A person, a country, a life—all seemed excuses for me to look up into the crystal-clear depths of the sky. I was Godiva, Iseult, Mélisande. I paused aboard a ship, in a forest, in a tower, and traveled across death while drinking up the night—I do not know of another potion. I know of no other hope than this for young girls asleep in glass boxes.

Notes for a Short Biography

III

He loved the whole city, but his favorite places were those with the secondhand stores and junk shops: 14th Street, Times Square, Little Italy, 2nd and 3rd Avenues in Lower Manhattan, and of course the Village.

Both *flâneur* and recluse, he worked very late into the night on his dreamy dioramas, where he combined his discoveries with echoes from his readings. It is no exaggeration to say that John Donne, Baudelaire, Dickinson, Nerval, Apollinaire, Rimbaud, Mallarmé, and Proust are as important to his boxes as the knickknacks he brought in from the street.

He had the bad habit of talking for hours on the telephone. His conversations, which were closer to monologues, scared off many friends.

His Journal includes an entry from the 1960s about reading *Ficciones* by Jorge Luis Borges.

Bande à Part
(*Mulberry Street*, 1967)

Almost always alone on the dirty sidewalks, the children—
with their wool hats and rubber boots, their yo-yos and hula-
hoops—play hopscotch, jump rope, eat lollypops, come and
go among adults who circulate without noticing them. It
looks like rain. The city grows dark and becomes more unreal,
especially Mulberry Street on the Lower East Side. Joseph
Cornell films the scene against a backdrop of tenement houses
where immigrants have always been crammed in together and
poverty fights against itself. From a pedestal, Mozart gazes at
the children—or rather, the bust of Mozart that occupies a
shop window crowded with plaster angels and other tasteless
items. Nothing else happens. It is already miracle enough
that someone has noticed them—transforming them into a
signifier that is open to things we will never know.

Sonate
C-Dur / Ut majeur / C major
KV 309

That night, as happened every night, the girl dreamed that she had been born an orphan, and that this circumstance—if it may be called that—drove her into a world within the world that to her looked like a beautiful circus, full of tiger-tamers, contortionists and fire-breathers. She had been given the role of Death. Her routine involved balancing on a rope, but she would become tangled in her own hair and, without fail, make a mortal leap into the impossible. For no apparent reason, she repeated the fall three times—and what is worse, with no one to watch. Love is an ancient art, impossible and cruel.

PÂLE

CÉLESTE

BLEU

LE

ATTAQUÉ

ONT

ABEILES

LES

The Symbolic Equation

Borges often recounted the scene where Harald Hardrada, the Norwegian Viking king, accompanied by the Duke of Tostig—brother and enemy of English King Harold Godwinson—receives a man in his camp, the day before battle, who calls himself an emissary of the king. What follows is a dance of shadows. To avoid the battle, the supposed emissary offers Tostig half the kingdom, and his Norwegian ally seven bits of land. Recognizing the emissary is his brother, Tostig refuses this vile offer and the battle that ensues affords Harald Hardrada the honor of dying in combat.

This happened around 1066.

Not far from there, in the Earldom of Coventry, Godgifu intercedes on behalf of her already plundered subjects, requesting that her husband, Duke Leofric, not raise their taxes. Her husband responds by offering her a challenge. He says he will grant her wish if she will ride naked through the streets of the village. And so, one morning, Godiva—*Good Eve*—beloved of the Virgin, protector of the defenseless—makes her passage along the cobblestones, accompanied by a terrible silence (the king has ordered everyone to leave the streets), and covered only by her hair like a sleeping Amazon. And without any warning, with no other witness than the first voyeur in history—that curious Peeping Tom—between horse and hair, an erotica spreads, encouraging pleasure, tolerance and unbridled freedom. This ride is among the most lucid exercises of human fantasy. It is also an invitation to travel and a profane prayer in favor of desire.

```
L A L A L A L A L A L A L A L A L A L A L
A V A V A V A V A V A V A V A V A V A V A
D I D I D I D I D I D I D I D I D I D I D
Y D Y D Y D Y D Y D Y D Y D Y D Y D Y D Y
G O G O G O G O G O G O G O G O G O G O G O
O G O G O G O G O G O G O G O G O G O G O G
D Y D Y D Y D Y D Y D Y D Y D Y D Y D Y D Y
I D I D I D I D I D I D I D I D I D I D I D
V A V A V A V A V A V A V A V A V A V A V A
A L A L A L A L A L A L A L A L A L A L A L A
```

(*Vaudevilles De-Luxe*, Circa 1940)

New York, Paris, Rome, interesting Sweden, a country called Marken, jungles, markets, views of the Far East: Something like panoramas filmed to entertain the tourists (real or imagined) we are. Here, too, the children are given priority, even when working, picking fruit or lifting bundles. They are like the glove that for a moment hides a wound—because it dazzles the pain. Such views are implausible; not recognizing the laws of cause and effect, time and space. There are lizards, views of the Piazza Navona, vintage book collectors along the Seine, Caribbean sugar harvesters, rice paddies. Boats— loaded with passengers—lurch along on a turbulent river, streetcars move very quickly—as if we were suddenly inside Dziga Vertov's dizzying film (*Man with a Movie Camera*, 1929). Sometimes the images move backwards or are upside down. Is it a factory? An aerial photo of the Eiffel Tower? The tip of Manhattan? Joseph Cornell's film collages, wrote Jonas Mekas, are the invisible cathedrals of the twentieth century.

s   he,   Miss

          boy   actress

      Emily   Dickinson

   fée   *fata*   fairies

f   a   t   u   m

(*Hans Christian Andersen Theater, Dance Index* No. 9, 1945)

Once there was a small box that a cobbler kept in the back of his workshop. The box was full of velvet cloaks for his most prized puppets—the King, the Queen and the Fairies. He would dress them in the cloaks when putting on a show with them in the little homemade theater—works that grew from the imagination of the boy he had once been.

Scene I

Prelude: Colors from a magic lantern. When the fanfare (*Rosemunde* by Franz Schubert) ends, the curtain opens.

Scene II

Allegro for strings by Ravel. Morning light. Thumbelina struggles against a giant beetle but is saved by a butterfly who takes her downstream, sailing on a leaf.

Scene III

Close up of Mrs. Night. In the dark foliage of this enigma, an ordinary nightingale breaks out in song. From this song, a flower soaked in moonlight is born, a *Wunderblume*.

Scene IV

Music from Albert Roussel's *The Spider's Feast*. A lead soldier watches as a ballerina wearing a white tutu approaches and touches him. When the tower clock strikes 12:00 o'clock, the ballerina and the lead soldier will perform a slightly sinful *pas de deux*.

Scene V

A tin box. Several toys soon emerge from it: Kings on horseback, a matchbox girl, storks in flight that carry a princess with them, several wind-up mice, a little mermaid like a Venus born from a seashell. They all start moving—reminding us of Méliès' cinematic magic.

Unfortunately, Eos with her rosy feet appears to the right and sneezes. A fine, invisible dust sprays from her nose—freezing all the characters in place for the GRAND FINALE.

Falling stars

      stars in the sky

          circus stars

             child stars

                movie stars

                   starlight

                      little stars

                          ****

                              ***

                                  **

                                     *

(Cloches à Travers les Feuilles, 1957)

In this festival of sad childhood, the ephemeral sings its song dressed in white. The park lights up—upward toward where everything barely lives: The pigeons, the leaves, the circles of light, the silence we don't see, beyond and before this the stars. We are then, once more, in a park. An unmistakable park in Manhattan; surrounded by skyscrapers, devoid of humans. Joseph Cornell watches, giving exact instructions to Rudy Burckhardt (who is in this case the one filming)—and spells out in his blind alphabet the broken images that continue—exactly—the duration of the piano piece by Debussy that he will use as the soundtrack. Something flutters in the heart of fear, and this is enough. Krazy Kat takes the mouse he loves—even though the rodent abuses him—out for a stroll in a wheelchair.

In the beginning, the Goddess of All Things arose, naked, from the Chaos. She was wooed by the wind and laid a silver egg from which the universe emerged. She was known as Wander without Limits or Brilliant Mother of Nothing, worshipped as Visible Moon in her three phases: as a damsel or girl, as a lusty nymph and as a soothsaying crone. So the girl on the white steed could be Isis or Ishtar or Iphigenia or even Helen of the Tree or the *petite Héloïse* when she was not yet nubile. Also who knows if this is not the blonde Andromeda, a child Cassiopeia or any of the other Pleiades, without breasts, that the gods place high above us in the sky like a musical toy.

Workshops of the Future

There were many of them in those years, especially in New York on the streets neighboring Times Square.

All sorts of small stands that featured a wide variety of amusements: Slot machines, pinball machines, five-cent thrills (Penny Dreadfuls), shooting galleries, punching-balls, wheels of fortune, and above all—Kinetoscopes. These were set in motion by inserting a coin, and presented miniature shows for the viewer—brief narratives running approximately 60 seconds that offered the spectator the strangest entertainments.

These optical skits—where the transcendental and the unalterable appeared together before him in the midst of platitudes—fascinated Joseph Cornell, as this is something we don't normally see, because it is inconsequential or merely ordinary.

Certain individuals, wrote Charles Simic, experience solitude and unhappiness as a kind of poetry.

The Art of Losing Isn't Hard to Master

That night, Joseph Cornell stopped work early. He seemed dissatisfied, as if he had missed something essential. Something told him the girl on the white steed, despite her calm or sad expression, was fleeing. But fleeing from what? Not from unjust men. That wouldn't be very interesting, he thought. Nor from the questions he asked her as an artist, since he himself didn't know what they were. That night, he prayed as well as he could in the language he could use; a plea in which he asked, strangely enough, for what he needed, not for what he wanted.

Our Lady of the Sphere, he said, Scepter of the Night, Goddess of the World's Autumns: Never grant me the art of reading omens. (For I prefer the enchantment of things I do not understand).

Allow me to bear uncertainty, to coexist with my glass and wood boxes—those traps that grasp hold of things (such as poems).

Do not allow anyone to take from this child her disheveled air of sleep, that look of being exiled from the world. Before and beyond the law, keep her this way—even, and above all, for me.

Gnir Rednow (1955)
(*Wonder Ring*)

Cornell didn't like the perspective of the L Train that Stan Brakhage filmed, under his direction. So he took the footage, turned the city around, put the train upside-down and projected everything from end to beginning—without forgetting to invert the letters in the title. The result is a hallucinatory rewind, a symphony in red, a riddle that the city brazenly displays the better to hide itself.

T h e E n d i s t h e B e g i n n i n g.

.G n i n n i g e b e h t s i d n E e h T

Toward a Minor Movie

We will never know if it is true. Friends and critics told the story like this: Since there was no television at that time, Joseph Cornell often came back from his work with rolls of old 16mm films he would find in old shops around the city. On those days, there were private film screenings at home: Cornell started up the projector, and he and his disabled brother would watch the show together. Among these films, all B-movies, one in particular seduced them. It was called *East of Borneo*, and had been directed in the 30's by a notable unknown. They watched it thousands of times, until they grew bored. Then Cornell went down to the basement, cut up the copy, and reedited the scenes, arranging them in a less predictable sequence. This would satisfy him, and his brother, for a while. He repeated the process several times (whenever he and his brother grew bored) and thus the film we know today, which Stan Brakhage has described as one of the greatest cinematographic poems of all times, was the product of a back-and-forth between entertainment and boredom, joy and disappointment—a game, after all, like all works of art. A meticulous game of chess played against the Black Queen who returns to stand, again and again, on the white square.

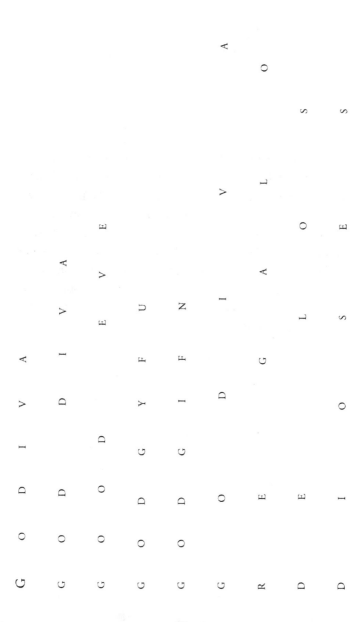

Notes for a Short Biography

IV

Like Raymond Roussel, who explored Africa without leaving the tent where he wrote *Impressions d'Afrique*, or Michel Leiris, the professional ethnographer who, in *L'Afrique Fantôme*, questioned the purpose of travel as a method for acquiring knowledge, Joseph Cornell is among those travelers fascinated with the idea of the stationary journey—the kind of travelers who are, in the first place, artists consuming images, taxonomists of reality. The imaginary journey and the journey as imagination are masterfully coordinated in the hermit of Utopia Parkway.

(Rose Hobart, 1936)

In this version of *The Thousand and One Nights*, a beautiful woman tells the story of another beautiful woman who tells the story of another beautiful woman in a pseudo-Arabian harem. There are merchants, perhaps, a loaded revolver, crocodiles and even an active volcano erupting at the same moment as an erotic scene that can't be seen. The woman could be a cloaked hunter (she has a safari hat) and the jungle a tapestry of her states of mind.

Late summer between fluffy cushions and half-moon shapes. Marimbas are playing, palm trees whistle, the volcano with its deranged music. The soundtrack magnifies our disconnection with what we see. Beautiful as the moon, the woman flirts with herself and at times with a little monkey that she caresses as if it were a little monkey. Close-up of a man in a turban, a sultan or vizier—connoisseur of dreamlike pleasures and of dreams more inadequate than arbitrary. The woman, untouchable as the breeze, more unsteady than the hidden pistol. Her white dress against the arches and Moorish battlements that repeat the impossibility of this story, of all stories.

In the end, death, as always, is life.

Sélavy.

The poster says: *East of Borneo*.

The film, a sort of neurotic Gothic, was going to be called *Tristes Tropiques*, in honor of Lévi-Strauss, who hated travel.

It was Joseph Cornell's first collage. Through a process of cutting and rearranging the material, he edited George Melford's B-movie down to 19 minutes, affirming, in passing, that what is essential to film is the visual—without narrative interfering. They say that Dalí, who was at Julien Lévy's gallery when they screened the film, suffered an attack of envy.

Ode   the   Other

An   to   of

Blue   Night   World

(Midnight Party, 1940)

A world of *freaks*, acrobats, trained seals that play the banjo or spin beach balls on their noses, blindfolded *Indians* who throw knives at a supposed captive, magicians—each in their own time and also at the wrong time—ballerinas and can-can dancers but all favoring *pointe* shoes, tutus, tulle, gauze, tiaras, the melodramatic sparkle of frilly hems and bodices. Also, curls are important. Small handbags. Shoes that pinch the feet when balancing on nothing.

the map

When I return to my castle of origin, I will write a nocturne with a *clair de lune* and call it *My Poetic Astronomy*. I will imbue it with the excitement of the night, as it has been recorded over centuries—with its priestesses, its crimes, its waters that cross the borders of the world and disappear into nothing. This has been my life. An excursion into untraveled terrain in order to hide myself, at last, in the music of words, and to remain unreachable to myself. I never managed to cry, or to love, or to plunder the facts. All I did was cross the sky in my imagination, like a tremor, leaving behind traces of the vivacious universe.

A Chorus Line

That day, the day when he discovered the small Godiva on the white steed, Joseph Cornell had been wandering for hours without finding anything—no object or image for him to take home and later obey as he would an accidental teacher.

And now that he has her in his hands, what is he thinking?

Nothing. That is, everything.

If he could reduce this vision down to zero, capture the excitement of this experience in ruins, he would be happy as a great failed artist.

Life, Fitzgerald wrote, is a process of breaking down.

That's it.

Who knows, if he stops collecting feelings, he might access the passion of what is to come—that is, what happens in between things, not in each particular thing. Perhaps he is given some miniature, some intact aftertaste of night, so that he may narrate death.

A Collector as Filmmaker

As if the movies were made for, and by, children.

Hence their brevity—none of the shorts longer than ten minutes.

Also, the delight in repetition, the desire for details, the impulse toward microscopic items and, in general, for all forms of openness—glass, windows, storefront displays— that allow a face, a bird, a bottle or an amoeba to be shown for contemplation.

Now you see it. Now you don't. One image fades, another bends or rather becomes inverted or unfolds from end to beginning. Moreover, it can stay fixed in place or enlarge itself as if in close-up mode, or even freeze inside a box. Who cares? Hierarchies do not exist in childhood time. Stigmas against anarchy do not exist. A sort of happy chaos, though a little bit grubby, imposes itself on the scene. The result is a *vanity fair* atmosphere where Imagination rules as queen and Desire digs a cave in the room of the impossible.

Our Angelic Ancestor
Charles Simic

Rimbaud should have gone to America instead of Lake Chad. He'd be 100 years old and rummaging through a discount store. Didn't he say he liked stupid paintings, signs, popular engravings, erotic books with bad spelling, novels of our grandmothers?

Arthur, poor boy, you would have walked the length of Fourteenth Street and written many more "Illuminations."

Poetry: Three mismatched shoes at the entrance of a dark alley.

In Joseph Cornell's library there were more than eight

volumes of stories and novels by   h a

n s   c   h   r   i   s   t   i

a   n   a   n   d

e   r   s

e   n

Sometimes he gives me apples that he says arouse poetic inspiration. Others he pulls up as if suddenly awakening and wishing to find the world, right now. All of this makes my white steed grow anxious: he groans about righteous souls, television, beer and, in general, about anything plotting against the memory of having a body. To everyone else, he is pleasant and quite intelligent. He knows that understanding is a mistake, that the darkness he most fears lives inside of him (not outside) and that his most essential task is learning to separate the word love from the word death.

Tristia

The moment he handled the image of the small Godiva, Joseph Cornell thought, perhaps, of the damage caused by old age. His long, thin fingers moved unhurriedly, accustomed as they were to working with celluloid. But his mind was elsewhere. The season, he thought, was no longer a favorable atmosphere for so many things. Why, on the other hand, was desire still intact? He looked around and saw only debris—edges and forbidden bedrooms, torment in the tired-out house. Afterwards, he looked again at the image. I am still a kind of music, he thought. A stubborn elegy, capable of capturing the intrigue of a human street. I can still, like Ovid, write uneven couplets about exile. This is not too much, nor too little.

From Joseph Cornell's Secret Library

Ernest, Max. *La femme à 100 têtes*, prologue by André Breton.

Contes de Fées. Imageries d'Epinal, 1850.

Paris Photo Album, 1910.

Apollinaire, Guillaume. *Le poète assassiné*.

The Complete Poems of Emily Dickinson.

Preston Peabody, Josephine. *The Book of the Little Past*.

Bernardin de Saint-Pierre, Jacques-Henri. *Paul et Virginie*, 1787.

La Science Amusante, 100 Expériences. Libraire Larousse, Paris, 1880.

Guest, Ivor. *The Romantic Ballet in England*.

Dillingham, Charles. *Globe Theatre*, 1880.

The Giant Golden Book of Mathematics.

Ante-Diluvian World – Organic Remains of a Former World, London, 1875.

Boys, C.V. *Soap Bubbles*, 1902.

Les Planètes. Paris, 1870.

Binder, Otto. *The Moon, Our Neighbouring World*, 1959.

Weather: A Guide to Phenomena and Forecast (301 full-color illustrations).

Ebb & Flow. *The Curiosities of the Sea Shore*.

Piaget, Jean. *The Language & Thought of the Child*.

Peele, Robert. *Christian Science, its Encounters with American Culture*.

Ross, Peter V. *Lectures on Christian Science*.

Wilbur, Sibyl. *The Life of Mary Baker Eddy*.

Baker Eddy, Mary. *Science & Health with a Key to the Scriptures*.

Laas, William. *Crossroads of the World: The Story of Times Square*.

Hobhouse, Christopher. *1851 & the Chrystal Palace*.

Thoreau, Henry David. *Walden*.

Proust, Marcel. À *la recherché du temps perdu*.

Nerval, Gérard de. Poèmes.

Moore, Marianne. *Poems*.

Coney Island Old Timers' Album & Directory (1848)

New York Hippodrome Souvenir Book

Movies for the Millions.

The Circus.

Etcetera.

Notes for a Short Biography

V

Like Emily Dickinson, Joseph Cornell was a figure firmly bound to the home. Single and solitary, as was she, he also took on the responsibility of caring for a family member, as she did, by looking after his disabled brother.

He shared things in common with Marianne Moore, the Brooklyn modernist poet who was his contemporary. We know Cornell admired her poetry (that was so much like the "soliloquies of a library clock," according to Mina Loy), and that they maintained a correspondence. Apart from that, they were both regular visitors to the Manhattan Zoo and built worlds with birds and animals, real and imaginary. What is still stranger: they were both faithful followers of Mary Baker Eddy, who wrote books about health and science and founded a Protestant cult, the Church of Christ, Scientist. Cornell was an active member from 1920 until his death in 1972.

Susan Sontag, Marcel Duchamp, Mark Rothko, Tennessee Williams and Robert Motherwell were, perhaps, her closest friends.

They say I was mute from birth, but I don't know for certain. My alphabet is made of doubts that keep piling up one on top of other like moonbeams from a lineage unfamiliar to me. I don't know if my name is Goda the Good; if my hair is a branch of golden grass; if I will remain naked for the rest of the fight; if fairies appeared at the moment of my birth; if someone will prepare a loving banquet for me and if I will then be able to bear having and not having at the same time. Sometimes I ask myself if I am really a doll, brought to life in someone's imagination. It isn't easy to be alive. Faith is a difficult passion.

Architectural Portrait of the Artist

There are ten hotels, like the Commandments. They are: 1) designed to increase repressed desires; 2) specialized in massages that stimulate the mind's sensuality and games played with infinity; 3) equipped with galactic stations around which small eclectic trains circle; 4) thematically organized, with attractions like the Forest of Four Seasons or the Garden of Tranquility; 5) exclusively for casual encounters (referred to, euphemistically, as *affairs*) where a living awareness of death—exacerbated by the distractions of routine—serves as the aphrodisiac; 6) open to those who cannot dream (since here they can enter the dreams of others); 7) built like small music boxes that take comfort in death itself; 8) illuminated with magic lanterns that, with just the click of a button, show us the intricate journey of who we, perhaps, are or will be; 9) filled with divinatory devices which offer answers as arbitrary as the questions asked; and finally one that 10) hides, in the most remote part of itself, a naked girl who awaits no prince. Her nudity, therefore, does not taint her innocence, nor does it justify the nervous confusion one feels upon looking at her.

These hotels could have appeared in Steven Millhauser's bewitching novel *Martin Dressler* or even in the pages of Italo Calvino, but their creation originates instead from a very brief book by Robert Coover, *The Grand Hotels of Joseph Cornell* (Burning Deck, 2002).

A kiss a prince a forest of thorns a damsel asleep a curse a spinning wheel a syntax of small sprouts a fetish a poem a castle's air a moving archive a white steed a Russian ballet a souvenir from some enchantment a puppet theater a jewelry box a *rosebud* a delicate family of signs a time forgotten in time a ragdoll a memento a great wise bird *all works of art are sleeping beauties waiting to be kissed by the viewers' imagination.*

Grand Hôtel de l'Univers

Hôtel du Grand Palais   Grand Hôtel Couronne

Grand Hôtel Îles d'Or   Hôtel Royal des Étrangers

Penny Arcade Hotel   Hôtel de l'Observatoire

Hôtel de l'Étoile   Cristal Cage Hotel

Grand Hôtel du Vésuve   Grand Hôtel Pléyades

Grand Hôtel La Mer   Hôtel Sémiramis

Ostend Hotel   Hotel Eden

Andromeda Hotel   Night Skies Hotel

Grand Hôtel Fontaine   Poor Heart Hotel

GRAND HÔTEL DE CHEZ MOI

His work, said John Ashbery, is like a small oasis
in the forbidden landscape of surrealist art.

John Ashbery

He always seemed a slow, profound
and impenetrable being: a sort of movable eternity.
Something like a farmer, attentive to the process of time,
who follows rhythms that aren't his,
that it is not his responsibility to understand
or even indicate.

Jonas Mekas (*attrib.*)

He admired the surrealists but didn't share
their tendency toward darkness.

André Pieyne de Mandiargues

"Now Voyager,
Sail Thou Forth to Seek and Find"

Whitman also saw poetry everywhere. To him New York seemed a "divine kaleidoscope," a treasure of poems to be unearthed.

Apollinaire found inspiration in pamphlets, catalogues, advertising posters (which he viewed as the poetry of our times).

Schwitters collected fragments of conversation and newspaper clippings.

Picasso, Arp, Duchamp, Ernst, de Chirico did the same.

As did T.S. Eliot and Ezra Pound.

Collage is the most important artistic innovation of the twentieth century. By placing value on what is commonplace (in all its forms, even garbage) and by giving random items the status of artistic objects, collage manages to eliminate the separation between art and life. It also succeeds in letting the imagination play games, encouraging cracks to form in the world; suspending reason, once again, to the benefit of desire.

A commotion in the North: Night struck its shield three times. Then nothingness became visible, and all around appeared helmets, swords, ethereal crowns for a queen—that is, indecipherable signs that the girl gathered up inside her insatiable saddlebag. This lasted only an instant, but it was long enough to bring together magnificent panoramas, aqueducts, springs, invisible chores, fleets of stars along with their shipwrecks and some other raptures. Only when she reached the Rock of Sorrow did the girl stop. She slowly opened her saddlebag and said: Everything starts living. Eternity begins.

Ultima Thule

Cornell's New York, it occurs to me, must have resembled the city John Cassavetes portrays in his film *Shadows* (1959).

An improvisation of a city, in black and white, complicated by the neon lights and saxophone music that, at once, attract and confuse the metropolis's underground, the question of race and the dream of travel—always forgotten, always on the verge of beginning again.

Shadows provides a prismatic shade, allowing Cassavetes to see what Cornell saw and, with this, to create his own handbook of melancholy and unease.

Like Cornell, Cassettes offers a dark tribute to the ghostly city.

The two live in a counterworld: They travel through it with their crafty suitcase, their own open fever—precisely toward what isn't seen (because it is visible).

Differences; however, exist: Whereas Cassavetes nominates money and sex as the core urban heartbeat, Cornell chooses nickelodeons and penny arcades, pianolas, music boxes, and the general air of an amusement park or fair.

This preference isn't free: It allows Cornell to rid himself of realism and surrealism's double plague. His city is a kind of Mechanical Museum with an otherworldly air that takes the present back to the mythical nineteenth century.

Notes for a Short Biography

VI

Between 1932 and 1945, Joseph Cornell left his job as a textile broker and, following a brief stint as a door-to-door refrigerator salesman, began working as a freelance designer for magazines like *Vogue*, *House and Garden* and *Dance Index*. Around this time, he met Marcel Duchamp and had his first solo exhibition in Julien Lévy's gallery. His script for *Monsieur Phot*—a movie not meant to be filmed, but rather, only to be imagined—is from 1933. That was also the year he created his first film-collage, *Rose Hobart*; continuing, through other mediums, his fascination with movie stars, opera divas, ballet dancers and, above all, girls or small nymphs.

Or perhaps the princess is sad, and this is why she's gone out on her white steed—to take a ride through the Forest of the Emotions. And in her nudity, which her hair hides completely, she seems to be saying: My body lives in my mind and doesn't know who it is. Or else: I have no time to play outside these words. Then she leaves, hidden in herself, toward what she will probably learn upon growing weary of traveling toward worldly seductions.

Pergolesi's Dog

Stan Brakhage has, on several occasions, described Cornell as a difficult friend and an artist who, like no other, knew how to go straight to the heart of amazement.

Recognized today as the most talented and prolific figure in North American experimental film, Brakhage died in Canada at the age of seventy, leaving behind almost 400 films—among them, one recording a birth (that of his first daughter); a scene unparalleled in the history of cinema.

We know that the two artists collaborated on several projects, and that one fine day they stopped speaking to each other altogether. Stan Brakhage revealed why: Cornell had been unable to forgive him for his ignorance about who Pergolesi was—let alone for never having heard of Pergolesi's dog.

If I were me, said the girl, if I did not have to live in your world with its infinite poses, its endless celebration of a non-existent past—what an intimate party I would hold, what quests. I would be my own animal in exile, my absolute music, my book about myself that I don't know how to read. Then I would show you things in their true ruin, including my nocturnal ritual with its irregular diction. What an unsustainable adventure!

Notes for a Short Biography

VII

- Duchamp and Cornell met in 1933, but their friendship really took off in 1942 when Duchamp traveled to New York as a World War II refugee.
- Duchamp was 16 years older than Cornell.
- In 1923, Duchamp announced to the world that he would permanently give up art and devote his life to chess.
- Earlier, in 1913, Duchamp had invented the readymade. Suddenly, anything could become art as long as it appeared in a museum and was signed by an artist.
- In 1936 Cornell, for his part, developed box shapes that captured, from the beginning, the introspections of an Intimate Diary.
- As soon as he had settled in New York, Duchamp solicited Cornell's help in assembling one of his own projects: *Boîte-en-valise* (Box in a Suitcase).
- *Boîte-en-valise* was considered the ideal accessory for an artist in exile. Inside that suitcase were other suitcases where Duchamp's key works were reproduced, in miniature.
- Cornell applied the idea of the readymade to his films. The important thing was not the filming itself but to "find" material and then participate, by altering it.
- 1980: Joseph Cornell's work appeared in a retrospective at the MoMA in Manhattan.

Beyond their differences, the two artists turned self-confidence and margins into a virtue. They questioned the very idea of art and made objects, that weren't considered artistic, glamorous long before art turned pop.

Hexahedrons of wood and glass,

    scarcely bigger than a shoebox,

        with room in them for night and all its lights.

               Octavio Paz, "Objects and Apparitions"
                  (Translated by Elizabeth Bishop)

                  a snowbox of wonders.

             a basket of gifts,

           to spy on each landing

         without breathing harder

       in the grainy light,

      step after step,

     To climb the belltower,

Stanley Kunitz, "The Crystal Cage"

"*De la Musique avant Toute Chose*"

(Some of Joseph Cornell's records,
found in his study at the time of his death)

A Field Guide to Bird Songs
The World's Rarest Music Boxes in High Fidelity
Jean-Louis Barrault, Readings of Baudelaire & Rimbaud
Mendelssohn, *Music for a Midsummer Night's Dream*
Mozart, *Piano Concerto in KV454*
Beethoven, *Symphony 1 in C Major*
Schubert, *Impromptus*
Three Great Tchaikovsky Ballets: Sleeping Beauty, Swan Lake,
The Nutcracker
Chopin, *Ballades*
Hayden, *Piano Sonatas*
Debussy, *The Complete Works for Piano*
Robert Frost, reading his own poems
Von Weber, *Preciosa*
Americana, for solo winds

There were no witnesses the first time I died: The angel I had been fighting with was myself. The second time, I had to learn to speak your silence but did not manage to create an object possessing either order or disorder, nor a proper or improper face. The third time, I climbed up to make the passage across your boxes and threw myself into your choreographies—to the south and the north of the future, without knowing that borders do not exist, and all acts of fleeing are an illusion. No one is free from these delays. Next time, I will desert you on the mouth.

An Aporia for Joseph Cornell
Richard Howard

Any apartment lobby is a necropolis,
every dresser drawer a forbidden city—
so much you taught me, intimidated, warned:
colors are trite, edges not to be trusted,
textures, behind glass, refuse to explain
a world where fate and God Himself have grown
so famous only because they have nothing to say.
The tiny is the last resort of the tremendous.
The tiny is the last resort of the tremendous.
The tiny is the last resort of the tremendous.
The tiny is the last resort of the tremendous.
The tiny is the last resort of the tremendous.
The tiny is the last resort of the tremendous.
The tiny is the last resort of the tremendous.
The tiny is the last resort of the tremendous.
The tiny is the last resort of the tremendous.

How to Fill the Imagination with a Solar Flower

When he arrived at the workshop and saw the stills of the tiny Godiva on the white steed lined up on the table, Cornell's assistant was stunned.

He thought the girl embodied a star crossing the sky, a true celestial body moving in slow motion and dragging her hair behind her as if it were the tail of a comet.

He looked again, and it was then he noticed that Godiva was looking in the direction of a boy, who was in turn watching her from another frame. The conclusion: Cornell had allowed himself to once again be captivated by the impossible romance between a young Nerval and an unattainable actress: Another *Rhapsody for Hedy Lamarr.*

Cornell suddenly approached, as if expecting a comment, and the assistant refrained from giving his opinion. He knew his master abhorred narrative of any kind and had been capable of eliminating any sequence that might produce one, even rejecting the film in its entirety.

A silence passed between the two men, like a gift. Cornell went away smiling. Of course there was a story of star-crossed lovers there. It was impossible for him to ignore this, as he was perpetually one himself.

Someone is spying on her. As if trying to reach her, to know who she was between the owl and the moon when she crossed a page of white epiphanies. *Peeping Tom* of the self, lucid witness, *n i h i l.* Being was perhaps suffering. Indeclinable. And the small Amazon knows it, and the one who is spying on her doesn't.

nihil   nihil   nihil

OBITUARY
Joseph L Cornell

Private services for Joseph L. Cornell, 69, an artist and sculptor, internationally known for his collages and constructions utilizing small boxes, will be held Saturday at Oak Hill Cemetery, Nyack, NY. He died Friday at his home in Flushing, Queens, of a heart attack. Cornell's work has been exhibited in Paris and at the Guggenheim Museum, the Whitney Museum, The Metropolitan, Carnegie Institute and Museum of Modern Art.

Dear Butterfly,

Yesterday I dreamed that an army of ants was performing a dance on white sand. The fight was fierce, perhaps also, futile because the enemy was nowhere to be found or didn't exist at all. One of them had a magic sword and she was faster any human. Another hurled javelins like one presenting a gift of love. Another brandished alphabets she had torn from the branches, and still another hid behind the invisibility helmet. But some swayed in the air, equipped with sudden wings, or encircled their leaders making small, high-pitched cries. They looked like small Amazons, driving the cars of their bodies with golden bridles, or like strange maidens about to lie down, splitting open in erotic postures. I awoke, crying profusely.

Dear Butterfly,

Anoche soñé con un ejército de hormigas que ejecutaban una danza espiral sobre
una extraña arena lisa. La lucha (era) situación y feroz. luna de ella
blandía una espada mágica, era mas vieja que un ser humano. Otra
la misma fabulosa, ... tenía la piel ... , el siguiente
... a ... ..., ... se columpia-
ban en el aire, daban detubibos alas, o rodeaban a las jefas con pequeño
grito alribulad... ② Parecían amazonas diminutas que eran dueñas del
campo de sus cuerpos en bordes de oro-... ... y se dirigían
hacia nuestra ella misma, o hacia la noble de la inevitable
madre, ...
... su ... ... por final yacían hendidas, en condición exótica.

② ... afrontaban la batalla x la batalla =

① Y ... inútil
... incomprensible x si el ausencia no estaba alreviste y acaso no existía.

③ Otra blandía alfabetos que había arrancado a las ramas y otra aún
se asomaba tras el yelmo de la invisibilidad.

④ ... ... incomprensible, ya ... ...
... ...

As if...
....
....
....
....
....
....
....
....……………the childhood of death
or the death of childhood ....

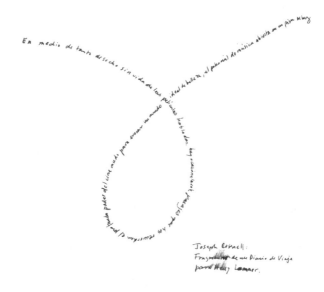

En medio de tanto desecho, sin vida de las películas habladas, hay momentos ocasionales que recuerdan el profundo poder del cine mudo para evocar un mundo ideal de belleza, el potencial de música abierta en una prima luminosa.

Joseph Cornell:
Fragmentos de un Diario de Viaje
para Hedy Lamarr.

In the midst of so much lifeless garbage from talking movies, there are occasional moments that remind one of silent film's profound power in evoking a world of ideal beauty, the potential for open music in premium light.

Joseph Cornell :
Fragments from a Travel Diary
for Hedy Lamarr

the window

CPSIA information can be obtained
at www.ICGtesting.com
Printed in the USA
BVHW040622060920
588167BV00004B/10

9 781628 973624